WISH YOU WERE HERE

Hans Ulrich Obrist

111 Artists
111 Notes

HENI PUBLISHING, LONDON

Wish You Were Here

Hans Ulrich Obrist

111 Artists
111 Notes

PREFACE

This is the second book based on my ongoing Instagram project in which I post handwritten messages created by the people I encounter in my life as a curator. The first volume, *Remember to Dream!* was published by HENI in 2023 and featured 100 of these notes, selected to demonstrate the sheer range of my collaborators. *Wish You Were Here* continues this approach and presents 111 new notes from a wholly different set of voices. It includes visual artists of all ages, geographies and backgrounds, along with other high-profile figures from many diverse fields such as architecture, film, music, literature, philosophy and technology.

Participants are invited to write whatever comes to mind on a Post-it, and can choose paper colour and writing tool. The words they offer range from universal idioms to the personal. Some speak to the concerns of our age and there are multiple musings on the future. While contributors are free to write in any language, many default to English, which is a reflection, perhaps, of the dominance of this *lingua franca* in the contemporary art world and on the Internet. Others reject words entirely and draw symbols or images. In this book, the notes are transcribed on the facing page in typographic approaches conceived by designer Irma Boom. These echo the energy of the writing and replicate specifics such as capitalisation, punctuation and position on the paper, to further reinforce how each individual approaches the same task in a unique way.

The eye is inevitably drawn to reading as the mind seeks to make sense of letters, words and phrases, yet the purpose of this project is also rooted in *how* these messages are rendered, more than what they say. For this is a campaign to save handwriting – an increasingly lost art in an era when keyboards and screens dominate written communication. In 2009, the novelist, critic, philosopher and semiotician Umberto Eco (1932–2016) told me about the significance of handwriting and his fear for its survival. In an article in *The Guardian* newspaper, he explained how learning to write manually teaches us to control our hands and develops hand-eye coordination. He reflected on how we must compose a phrase mentally before transmitting it:

there is no instant delete or undo function for the handwritten word. He even suggested that the resistance of pen and paper, as physical materials, slows us down and makes us think more than typically occurs when we type with our fingertips.

It was 13 years ago, when I was pondering a curatorial structure to engage with the burgeoning Instagram platform, that the epiphany occurred to unite the analogue and the digital. During a holiday with the artist-poet Etel Adnan (1925–2021), artist Simone Fattal and my partner, the artist Koo Jeong A, I saw Etel writing poems in a notepad and was struck by the splendour of her script. In an interview with her in 2011, she commented that, 'Something written by hand says more than just words – it reflects a psychological state'. This thought stays with me as I continue to upload the resolutely human-made into an online realm where AI-generated content increasingly proliferates.

As I wrote in the preface to the first volume, 'My handwriting project is an archive, a compendium of the handwritten form in the digital age. It shows beauty in the fact that human beings never have the same handwriting.' As it evolves through time, the whole project also functions as a memorial to those who have since died. Once transmitted into book form, the notes become even more solidly fixed in history: books being a medium that has endured for hundreds of years already. The book's title comes from the late Pope.L (1955–2023), a pioneering artist who passed too soon.

Hans Ulrich Obrist, April 2025

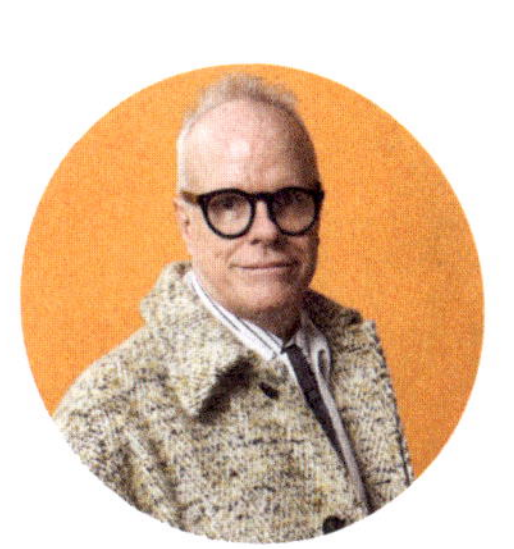

HANS ULRICH OBRIST

ARTISTS

1. Akomfrah, John
2. Anadol, Refik
3. Applebroog, Ida
4. Astakhishvili, Tolia
5. Atkins, Ed

6. Baghramian, Nairy
7. Barney, Matthew
8. Barrington, Alvaro
9. Baselitz, Georg
10. Beeple
11. Boeri, Stefano
12. Bradford, Mark
13. Brown, Cecily
14. Buterin, Vitalik

15. Calfuqueo, Seba
16. Chong, Heman
17. Cixous, Hélène
18. Clemente, Francesco
19. Copson, Matt

20. Dean, Tacita
21. Delany, Samuel R.
22. Devlin, Es
23. Diagne, Souleymane Bachir
24. Diller, Liz
25. Dine, Jim
26. Ducrot, Isabella

27. Ettinger, Bracha L.

28. Gordon, Kim
29. Gormley, Antony
30. Gray, Jon
31. Grosse, Katharina
32. Guadagnino, Luca

33. Haacke, Hans
34. Halsey, Lauren
35. Han, Byung-Chul
36. Herndon, Holly
37. Hershman Leeson, Lynn
38. Herzog, Jacques
39. Hicks, Sheila
40. Himid, Lubaina
41. Ho Tzu Nyen
42. Hopinka, Sky

43. Iglesias, Cristina
44. Imhof, Anne
45. Ishag, Kamala Ibrahim
46. Ix Shells

47. Jackson, Suzanne
48. Juliano-Villani, Jamian
49. Julien, Isaac

50. Katz, Alex
51. KAWS
52. Kelly, Mary
53. Kéré, Francis
54. Kid Cudi
55. Kim Hyesoon
56. Kluge, Alexander
57. Kojima, Hideo
58. Koons, Jeff

59. Lacy, Suzanne
60. Lanthimos, Yorgos
61. Leaf, June
62. Lee, Seung-taek
63. Lee Bul
64. Ligon, Glenn
65. Lin, Maya

66. Matsutani, Takesada
67. McCarthy, Paul
68. Mehretu, Julie
69. Mitchell, Tyler
70. Morris, Sarah
71. Murillo, Oscar

72. Nomata, Minoru
73. Notley, Alice

74. Oehlen, Albert
75. Ontani, Luigi
76. Oudolf, Piet

77. Patil, Amol K
78. Pessoa, Solange
79. Pistoletto, Michelangelo
80. Polachek, Caroline
81. Pope.L

82. Rego, Paula
83. Reyes, Pedro
84. Rodgers, Nile
85. Rovelli, Carlo
86. Rushdie, Salman
87. Ruthenbeck, Reiner

88. Sala, Anri
89. Saudi, Mona
90. Sebidi, Helen
91. Sharif, Hassan
92. Sherald, Amy
93. Siza, Álvaro
94. Skepta
95. Stamets, Paul
96. Swinton, Tilda

97. Taburet, Pol
98. Tadáskía
99. Teller, Juergen
100. Terrazas, Eduardo
101. Trecartin, Ryan
102. Trockel, Rosemarie
103. Tuten, Frederic

104. Uecker, Günther

105. Valcárcel Medina, Isidoro
106. Vally, Sumayya
107. Vezzoli, Francesco

108. Wales, Jimmy
109. Waters, John
110. Wenders, Wim

111. Yang Fudong

The Most Remarkable

Thing Is The Return Of

FORM

But in a new guise .

JOHN AKOMFRAH

The Most Remarkable
Thing Is The Return Of
FORM
But in a new guise.

John AKOMFRAH.

JOHN AKOMFRAH

Art is humanity's capacity of imagination!

Refik Anadol

Art is humanity's capacity of imagination!

Refik Anadol

REFIK ANADOL

I feel like an empty
house inhabited
by hungry tenants
Ida

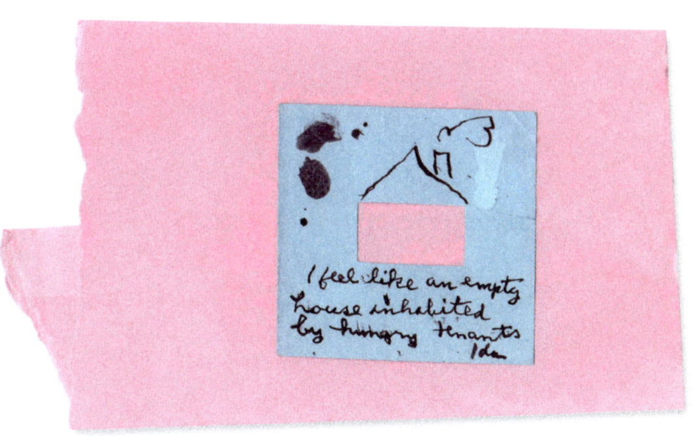

IDA APPLEBROOG

I wanted to write

and I drew

წყლა მინდოდა
და დავხატე

TOLIA ASTAKHISHVILI

THE FUTURE IS A GENEROUS

SANDWICH

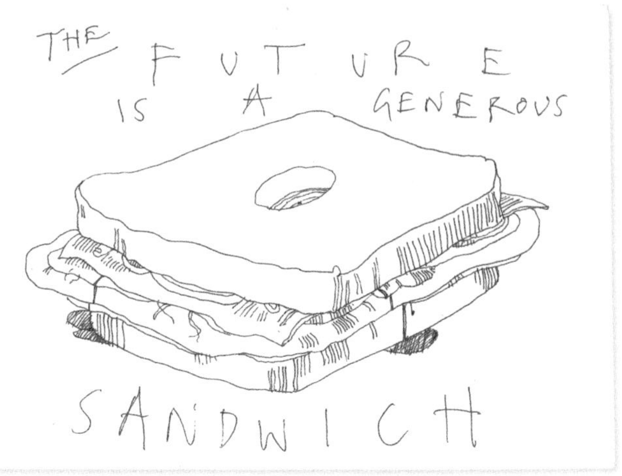

ED ATKINS

Eraser

NAIRY BAGHRAMIAN

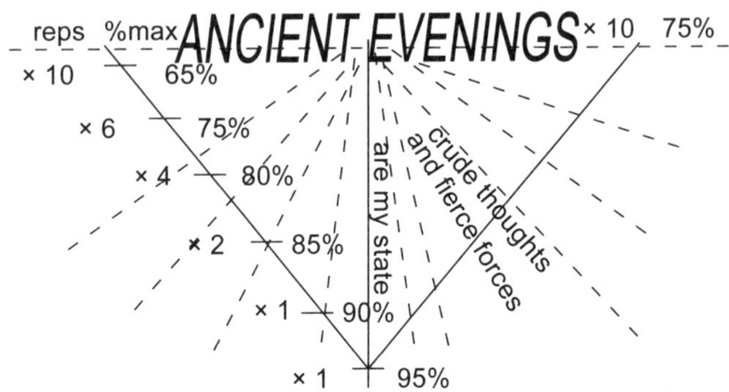
ANCIENT EVENINGS
reps
%max
× 10
65%
× 6
75%
× 4
80%
× 2
85%
× 1
90%
× 1
95%
× 10
75%
are my state
crude thoughts
and fierce forces

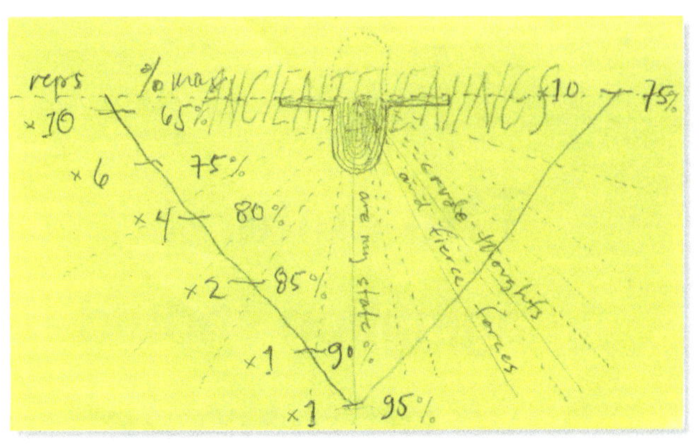

MATTHEW BARNEY

+-+-+

The cultural imagination should have no margins only live in it

+ - + + - +

ALVARO BARRINGTON

Art is Image / Reflection

G. Baselitz

Kunst ist
Schrift
G. Baselitz

GEORG BASELITZ

i don't believe there is any art that is any "better" or "worse" than any other art. the only thing that matters is the impact it has on you.

"beep le"

i don't believe there is any art that is any "better" or "worse" than any other art. the only thing that matters is the impact it has on you.

"beeple"

BEEPLE

IN THE FUTURE

NO EVENTS

ONLY STORIES

STEFANO BOERI 9 OCT 2014

IN THE FUTURE
NO EVENTS
ONLY STORIES

STEFANO BOERI 9 AGO. 2016

STEFANO BOERI

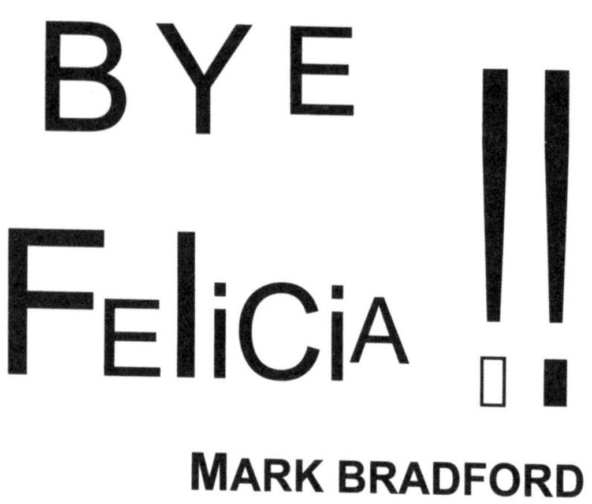
BYE
FeliCiA !!
MARK BRADFORD

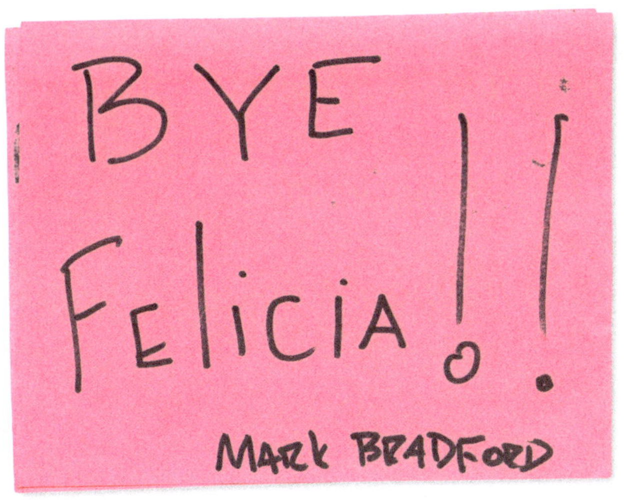

MARK BRADFORD

Painting is a way

of staying in the

moment forever

Painting is a way
of staying in the
moment forever

CECILY BROWN

(i) The world computer.

(ii) A system where anyone can interact with each other over an open network, and know that the interactions will play out according to the exact rules that the participants agreed on ahead of time.

vitalik

(i) The world computer.

(ii) A system where anyone can interact with each other over an open network, and know that the interactions will play out according to the exact rules that the participants agreed on ahead of time.

VITALIK BUTERIN

My_spirit_inhabits another_body

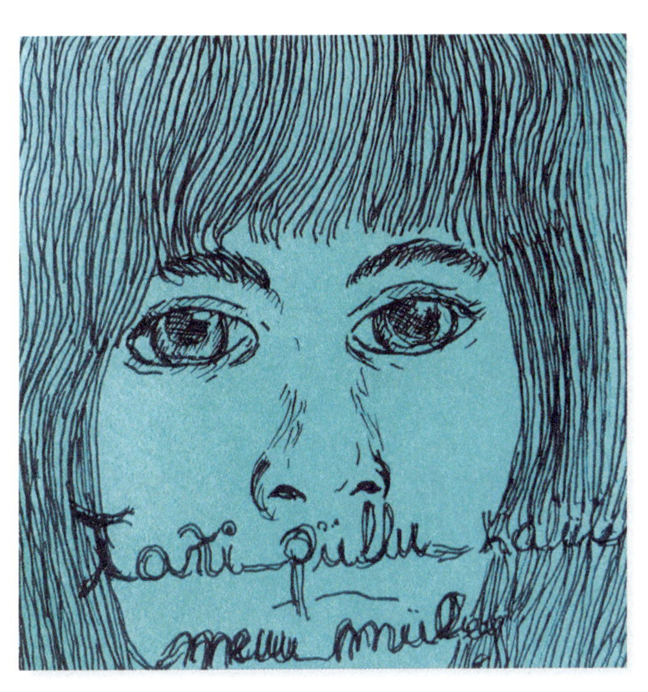

SEBA CALFUQUEO

Never , A Dull Moment

Never, A Dull Moment

HEMAN CHONG

Am I the last line of this story or the
first one of the story that I will never know?

? H?éle?ne Cixous with
Haya and Isha

17

Suis je la dernière ligne de cette histoire ou la première de l'histoire que je ne connaitrai jamais ?

?

Hélène Cixous avec Haya et Isha

HÉLÈNE CIXOUS

WITNESS

THE CONTINUITY

OF

DISCONTINUITY

(FRANCESCO CLEMENTE)

ॐ

WITNESS
THE CONTINUITY
OF
DISCONTINUITY
(FRANCESCO CLEMENTE)
ॐ

FRANCESCO CLEMENTE

REJOICE!
FOR THERE'S
NOTHING LEFT
ON A MORROWLESS
DAY.

REJOICE!
FOR THERE'S
NOTHING LEFT
ON A MORROWLESS
DAY.

MATT COPSON

$$\frac{\text{chaos}}{\text{chance}} = \text{process}$$

$$\frac{\text{chaos}}{\text{chance}} = \text{process}$$

TACITA DEAN

Du Bois said that the problem of the color-line would be the problem of the 20th Century ; the problem of misinformation will be the problem of the 21st Century .

— Samuel R. Delany

De Bois said that the problem of the
color-line would be the problem
of the 20th century; the problem
of missinformation will be the
problem of the 21st century.

— Samuel R. Delany

SAMUEL R. DELANY

"Thing number one :
The Earth is Madly in Love
with you: You need to
Participate in the Romance"
Es Devlin: quoting Leah Penniman:
Farming while Black .

"Thing number one:
The Earth is Madly in Love
with you: You need to
Participate in the Romance"
Es Devlin: quoting Leah Penniman:
Farming while Black.

ES DEVLIN

The philosopher I attach myself to is the one from whom I learn what I think .

Le philosophe auquel je m'attache est celui qui m'apprend ce que je pense.

SOULEYMANE BACHIR DIAGNE

I PREFER TO DO THINGS
I'M TOTALLY UNQUALIFIED TO DO .

Liz Diller

I PREFER TO DO THINGS
I'M TOTALLY UNQUALIFIED TO DO.

Liz Diller

LIZ DILLER

My oh My , How

YEARS have

WHIZZED PAST,

although I never thought they stood still .They are always moving like the big locomotive , so chocked full of energy . *Jim Dine*

My oh My, HOW
YEARS have
WHIZZED PAST,
although I never
thought they stood
still. They are always
moving like the
big locomotive,
so chocked full of
energy. Jim Dine

JIM DINE

"The decorative quality
of writing is
fading away, just as it happens
with fabric."

Isabella Ducrot

19. 6. 2023

"Il carattere decorativo delle sintesi è stato lasciato, come accade al tessuto"

Isabella Ducrot

13, 6, 2023

ISABELLA DUCROT

The twenty-first
    centure
will be com-passionate
    or
will   not   be

In   carriance   —BRACHA

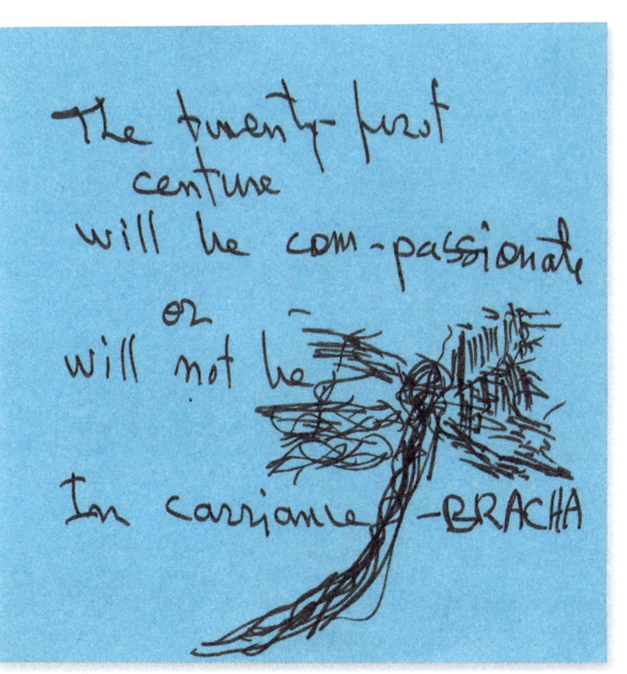

BRACHA L. ETTINGER

To punk or not to punk!

Kim G.

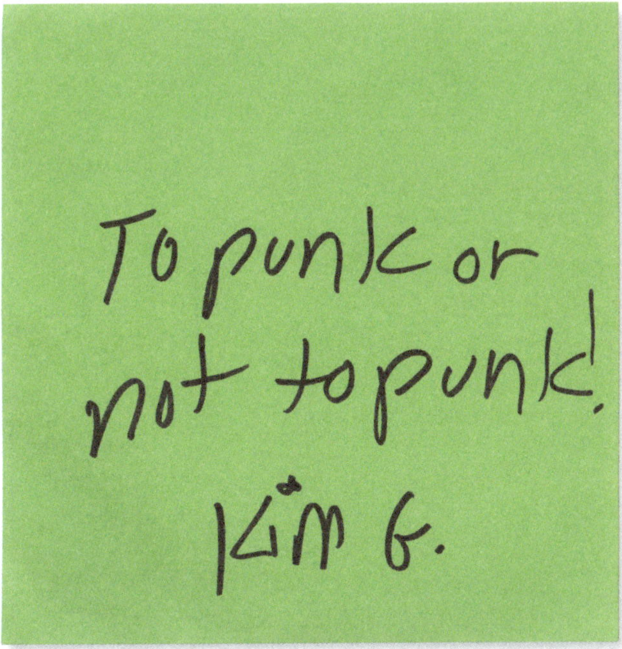

To punk or
not to punk!
Kim G.

KIM GORDON

the only permanence

is change

Antony.

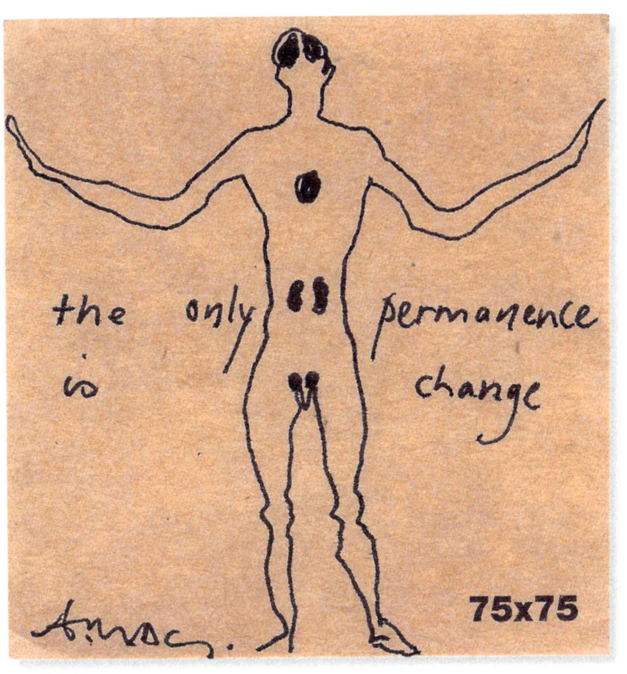

ANTONY GORMLEY

Stay Sturdy

&

WORTHY

J~ G

Stay Sturdy
&
WORTHY
J~ G

JON GRAY

Rebellious eyes

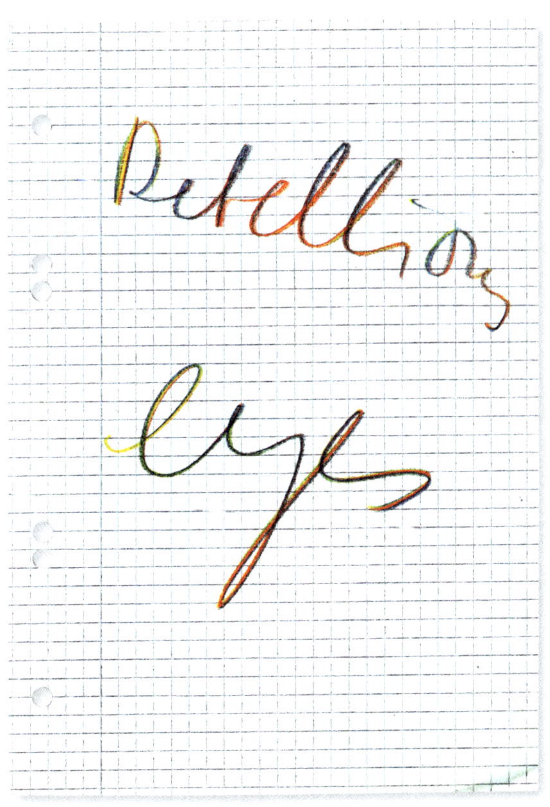

KATHARINA GROSSE

BRIGHTER THAN
THE MAGNESIUM
FLASH
,
THE LIGHT WITHIN

EMF

Luca
Guadagnino

PIÙ FORTE DEL
LAMPO AL
MAGNESIO,
LA LUCE INTERIORE

EMF

Luca
Guadagnino

LUCA GUADAGNINO

We (all) are the people

We (all) are the people

HANS HAACKE

THOU SHALL NOT

FOLD !♡

Lauren Halsey

THOU
SHALL
NOT
FOLD!

LAUREN HALSEY

A star

probably still has Light .

Nothing ,

nothing is lost .

Paul Celan

Ein Stern
hat wohl noch Licht,
Nichts,
nichts ist verloren.

Paul Celan

BYUNG-CHUL HAN

The children
made us.
Holly Herndon

The children
made us.
Holly Herndon

HOLLY HERNDON

I hope when you read

this on instagram you

experience a sexual sensation!

Lynn Hershman Leeson

I hope when you read
this on instagram you
experience a sexual sensation!

LYNN HERSHMAN LEESON

The hand writes

as it wants

the hand writes
as it wants

JACQUES HERZOG

curiousity
killed
the Cat

curiousity
killed
the cat

SHEILA HICKS

Do you
want
an
easy
life ?

LUBAINA x

Do you
want
an
easy
life?

LUBAINA x

LUBAINA HIMID

READ:

"Against Elections"

by David Van Reybrouck

READ:

"Against Elections"

by David Van Reybrouck

HO TZU NYEN

let us float

over the silty

sorrows of

mountains slowly

crumbling away.

– SH

let us float
over the silty
sorrows of
mountains slowly
crumbling away.

– SH

SKY HOPINKA

For Nature
to grow in
every direction

For Nature
to grow in
every direction

CRISTINA IGLESIAS

Anne Imhof

brand NEW Gods

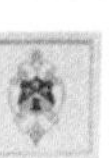

GRANGE STRATHMORE HOTEL

41 Queen's Gate Gardens, London SW7 5NB
Telephone: 020 7584 0512 Facsimile: 020 7584 0246
Email: strathmore@grangehotels.com Internet: www.grangehotels.com

brand NEW Gods

ANNE IMHOF

Art is life And

no less than that

Kamala Ibrahim Ishag

— الفن هو الحياة
ليس اقل منها

KAMALA IBRAHIM ISHAG

Bend!

I think is natural

To be a machine

IX Shells

: . . : . . . :

Bend!

I Think is natural

To be a machine

IX Shells

We should be living
in Natures way . . .
but we are
in Natures way .

Suzanne Jackson

We should be living
in Natures Way...
but we are
in Natures Way.

Suzanne Jackson

SUZANNE JACKSON

THE WORLD'S GREATEST PLANET ON EARTH

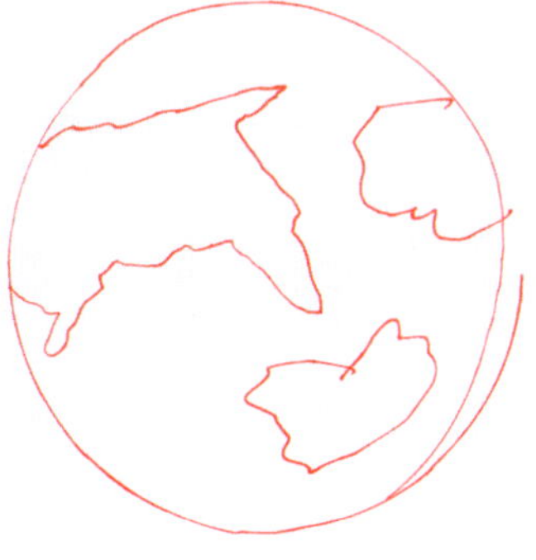

JAMIAN JULIANO-VILLANI

A MATTER OF ✓ Life

✓ Death

WE NEED A NEW REFUGE NOW !

Isaac Julien

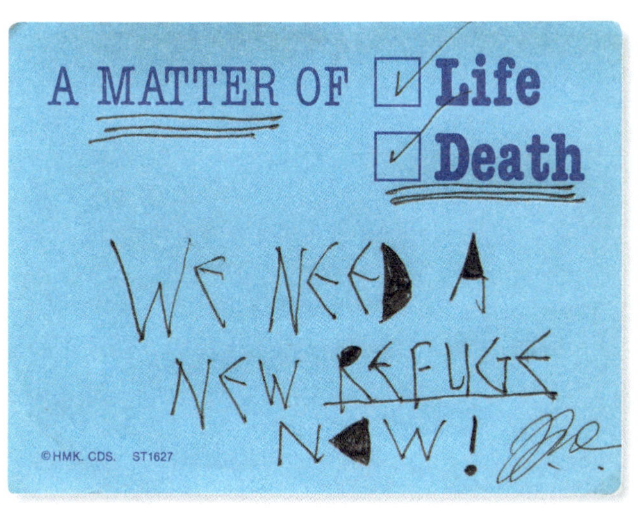

ISAAC JULIEN

*I like to make an image
that is so simple you
can't avoid it and so
complicated you can't
figure it out*

Alex

I like to make an image
that is so simple you
can't avoid it and so
complicated you can't
figure it out

Alex

ALEX KATZ

NEW FICTION ..

K A W S .. 21

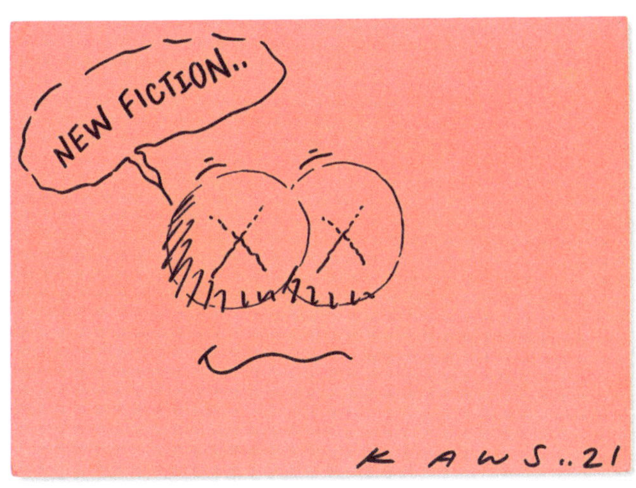

KAWS

Peace is the only shelter.

MaryKelly

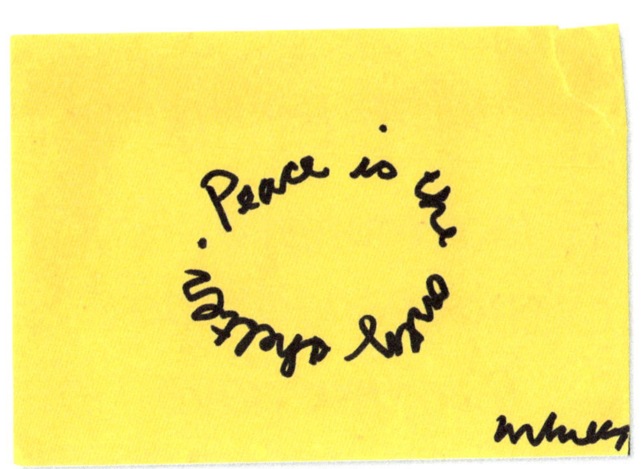

MARY KELLY

FRANCIS KERE

The fallen

leaves have
nourished the
tree that gave
its life to this
piece of paper
so, Respect !

Hey my friend Hou !

The fallen leaves have nourished the tree that gave its life to this piece of paper. So, Respect!

FRANCIS KÉRÉ

Hey my friend you!

FRANCIS KÉRÉ

Music is pure
l ife in sonics.
Follow the vibes!

Kid Cudi

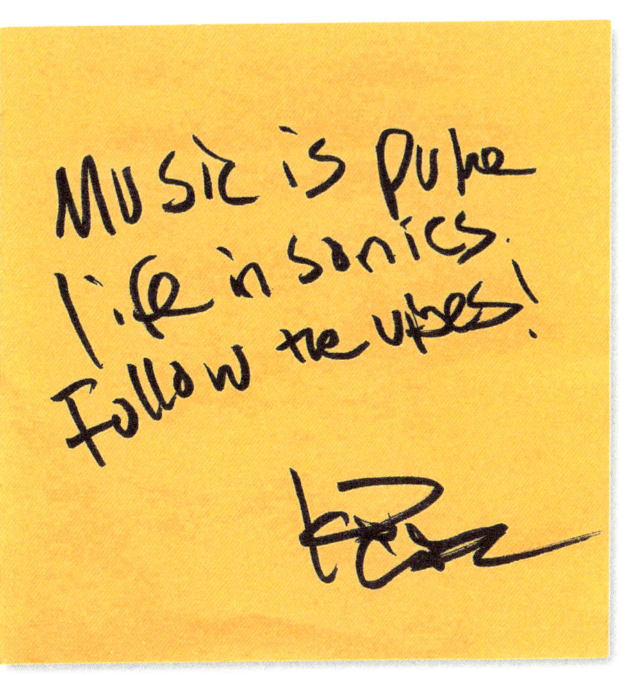

KID CUDI

My echoes and your echoes
meet and chatter
forever in a desert.

Kim Hyesoon
Sep. 4. 2022

내 메아리가 당신의
메아리를 만나 영원히
떠드는 사막이 있다.

Kim Hyesoon
Sep. 4. 2022

100% 사탕수수로 만들어진 친환경 종이입니다.
This paper bag is made from eco-friendly sugar cane bagasse.

KIM HYESOON

“ The revolution is a creature full of surprises ”

„Die Revolution ist ein Lebewesen voller Überraschungen"

ALEXANDER KLUGE

MOST OF THE THINGS
CONSIDERED IMPOSSIBLE
ARE ACTUALLY POSSIBLE
KOJIMA HIDEO

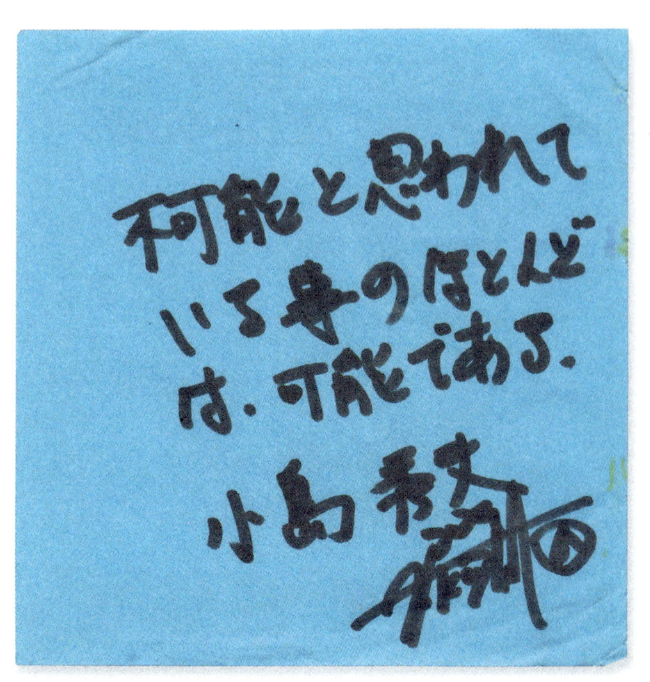

HIDEO KOJIMA

METAPHYSICS
THE RIGHT HERE NOW

AND
THE ETERNAL

METAPHYSICS

THE RIGHT HERE NOW

AND

THE ETERNAL

9/12/16

JEFF KOONS

Computers ruined my handwriting

Suzanne Lacy

Computers ruined
my handwriting

Suzanne Lacy

SUZANNE LACY

Rebellion is not always the right thing . Following the rules is not always the right thing. You have to think for yourself and identify the things that don't work for you .

Yorgos Lanthimos

Rebellion is not always the right thing. Following the rules is not always the right thing. You have to think for yourself and identify the things that don't work for you.

Yorgos Lanthimos

YORGOS LANTHIMOS

BE BRAVE

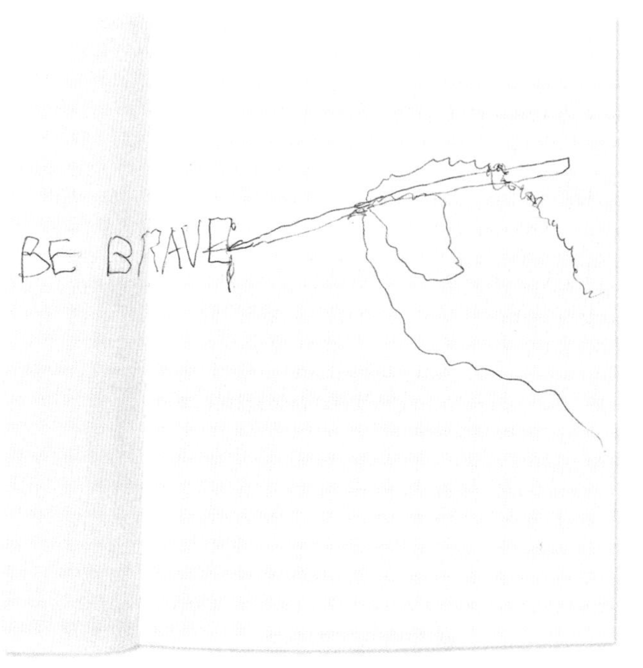

JUNE LEAF

I saw the world upside down.

I thought the world

upside down.

I lived the world upside down.

Seung-taek Lee

나는 세상을
거꾸로 보았다
거꾸로 생각했다
꺼꾸로 살았다

이승택

SEUNG-TAEK LEE

THERE IS NO DELAY

ONLY DISTANCE

– LEE BUL –

데어 이즈 노 딜레이
온리 디스턴스

-이불-

~~Gilbert & George~~

Lee Bul

There is no delay,
There is only distance

LEE BUL

"It was...
It was the best ...
It was the best of times.
It was.. .
It was the worst ..·.
It was the worst of times. "

Glenn Ligon

"It was...
It was the best...
It was the best of times.
It was...
It was the worst...
It was the worst of times."

Glenn Ligon

GLENN LIGON

I like to

think with

my hands .

M L

I like to

think with

my hands.

MYL

MAYA LIN

HEART

t
a
k
e
s
a
d
a

matsutani

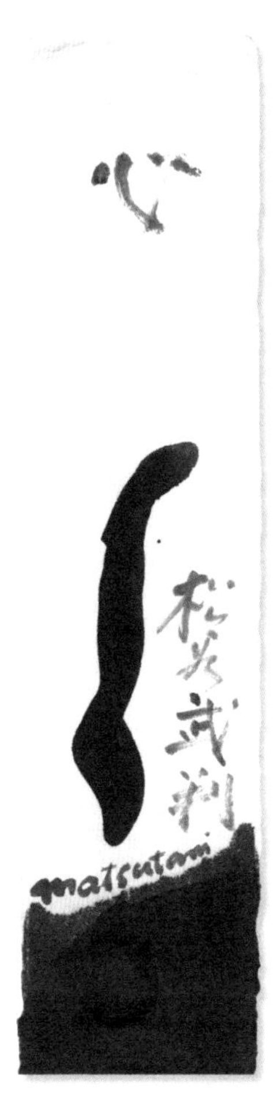

TAKESADA MATSUTANI

Paul McCarthy

This IS NOT The END yeT

PAUL McCARTHY

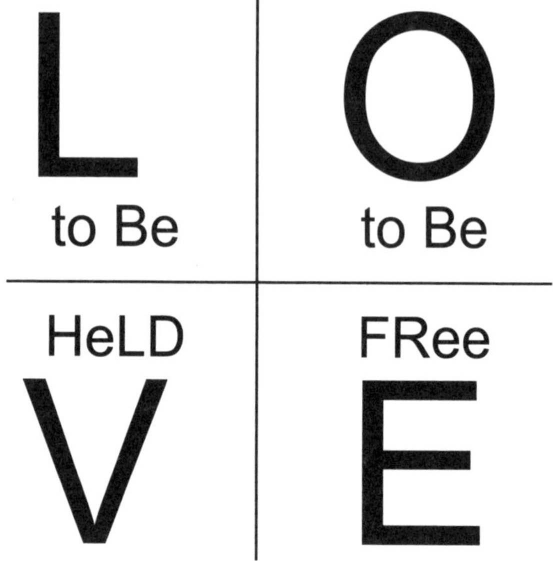
L
to Be
O
to Be
HeLD
V
FRee
E

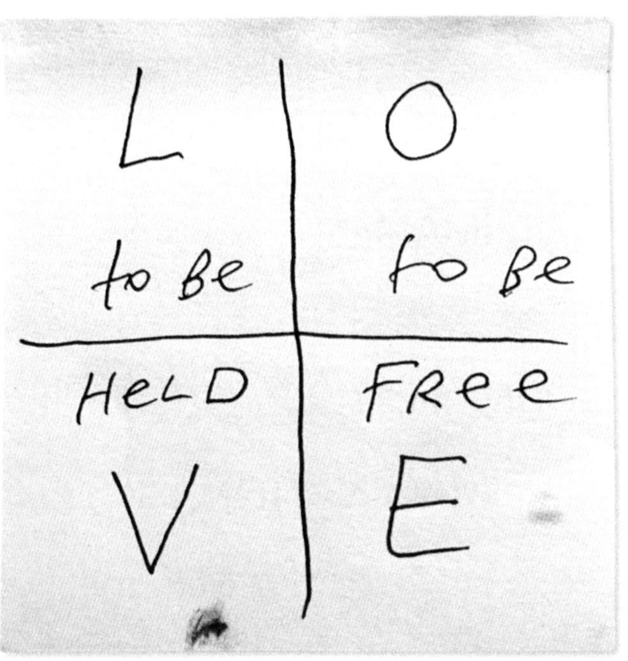

JULIE MEHRETU

INFINITE

IMAGES

=

INFINITE

IMAGINATIONS

Tyler Mitchell

INFINITE IMAGES = INFINITE IMAGINATIONS

Tyler Mitchell

TYLER MITCHELL

THERE EXISTS SOMETHING
BETWEEN US THAT IS
BETTER THAN YOU AND
THAT IS BETTER THAN ME .
IT IS A PRECIOUS STONE .

S M

' ALEXANDER KLUGE ' [told to Sarah Morris]
IN FINITE AND INFINITE GAMES

THERE EXISTS SOMETHING
BETWEEN US THAT IS
BETTER THAN YOU AND
THAT IS BETTER THAN ME.
IT IS A PRECIOUS STONE.

SM

'ALEXANDER KLUGE' IN
FINITE AND INFINITE GAMES

SARAH MORRIS

Can we pls undo Self

Segregation.

Can we pls undo Self
Segregation.

OSCAR MURILLO

Insufficiency

is the source of creation.

Minoru Nomata

Insufficiency

is the source of creation.

Minoru
Nomata

MINORU NOMATA

Hear that heroic
big land music ?

Alice Notley
3/27/22
Paris

Hear that heroic
big-land music?

Alice Notley
3/27/22
Paris

ALICE NOTLEY

make a selfportrait !

Albert Oehlen

make a selfportrait!

Albert Oehlen

ALBERT OEHLEN

Neo & neon

Contemporary

Extemporaneous

Neophyte

vacant

derelict

refugee unreal

unpredictable loyal

Ontani

Art Elsewhere

Hurrah

Neo & neon
contemporaneo
Estemporaneo
Neofito
afitto
derelitto
profugo irreale
aleatorio
Ontani

LUIGI ONTANI

I What can we put in a day

Piet Oudolf

What can we put in a day

Piet Oudolf

PIET OUDOLF

they both dance together

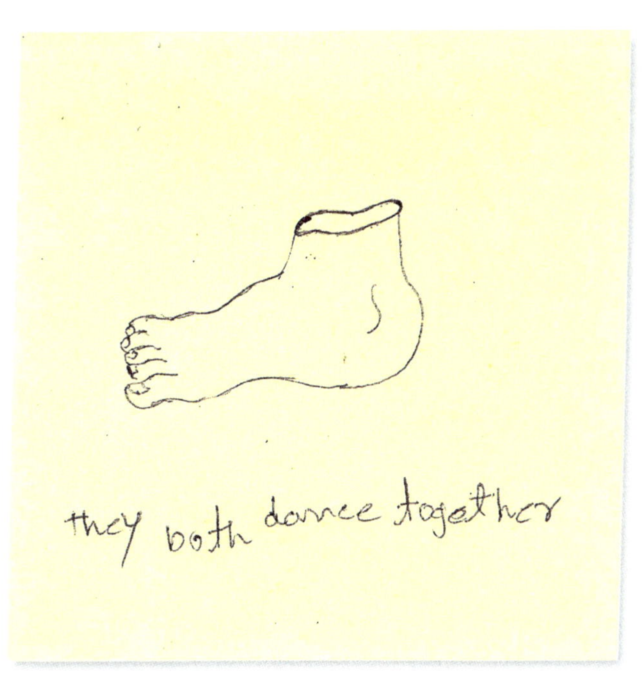

AMOL K PATIL

" Art is an experimental exercise of freedom "

(Mario Pedrosa) – Solange Pessoa

"A arte é o exercício experimental da liberdade"

Solange Pessoa - Mário Pedrosa

SOLANGE PESSOA

I am
the robot

the robot
is me

Pistoletto

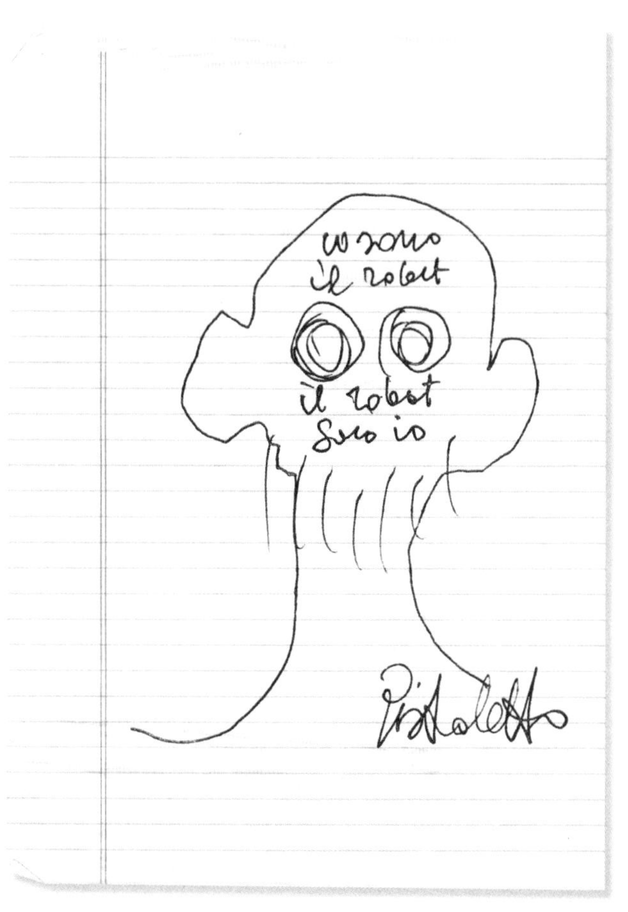

MICHELANGELO PISTOLETTO

the newness
is
the youness

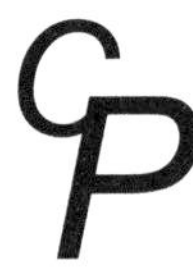

the newness
is
the youness

C.

CAROLINE POLACHEK

WISH YOU WERE HERE

Pope.L

POPE.L

You don 't get better you
just get better at it

Paula Rego

[quoting Victor Willing]

You don't get better you
just get better at it
Paula Rego

PAULA REGO

YOU'LL FIND THE FORMULA, AS LONG AS YOU KEEP YOUR MIND FRESH !

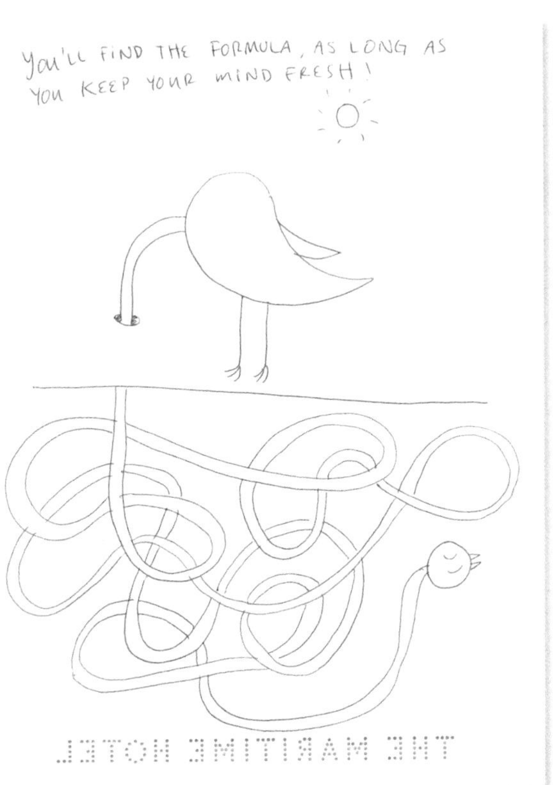
YOU'LL FIND THE FORMULA, AS LONG AS
YOU KEEP YOUR MIND FRESH!
THE MARITIME HOTEL

PEDRO REYES

WE ARE

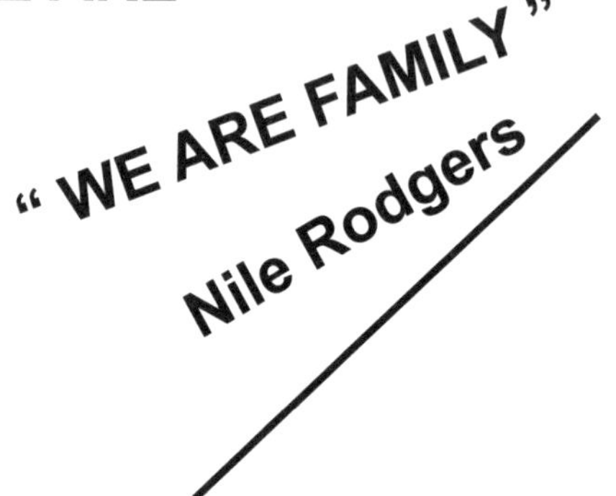

We ARE

"WE ARE Family"

Nile Rodgers

NILE RODGERS

$$A_{\vec{j}} = \sum_l 8\pi\hbar G\gamma\sqrt{j_l(j_l+1)}$$

$$Y_\gamma|j,m\rangle = |\gamma j, j; j, m\rangle$$

$$W(\psi) = P_{SL2C}Y_\gamma\psi(\mathbb{1})$$

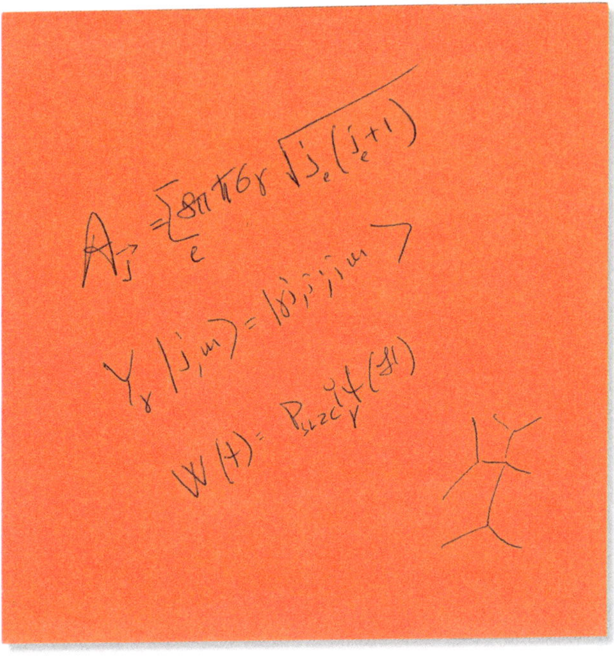

$$A_{\vec{j}} = \sum_e 8\pi \hbar G \gamma \sqrt{j_e(j_e+1)}$$

$$Y_\gamma |j, m\rangle = |\gamma j, j; j, m\rangle$$

$$W(\ell) = P_{SL2C}\, Y_\gamma f(\ell)$$

CARLO ROVELLI

Milan Kundera said, more or
less, that the realist tradition
in literature is exhausted .
So the question is, “what is
there left to do?”
And the answer is,
“Everything.”

Milan Kundera said, more or less, that the realist tradition in literature is exhausted. So the question is, "what is there left to do?" And the answer is, "Everything."

SALMAN RUSHDIE

Happiness

R. Ruthenbeck

Glück

R. Ruthenbeck

REINER RUTHENBECK

00:00

" Dreaming of another era "

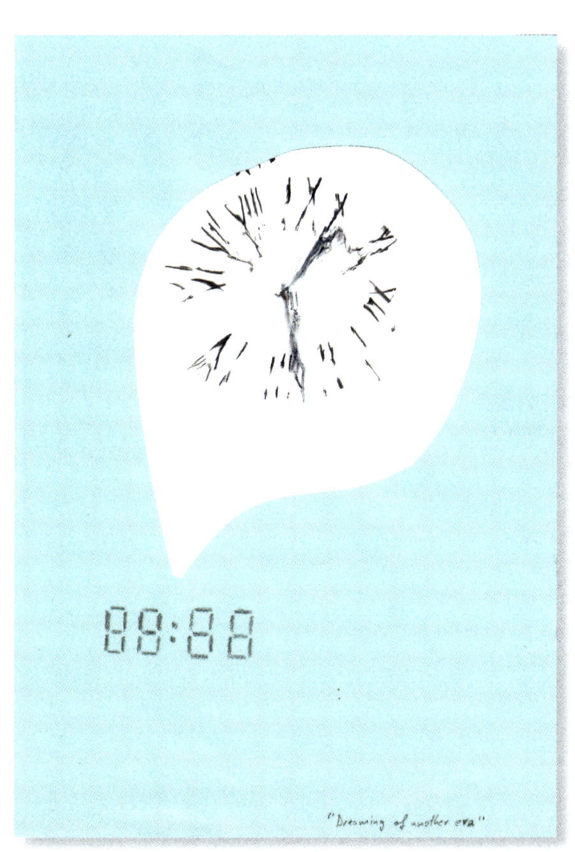

ANRI SALA

And from where do you obtain

all this joy

You who are haunted with light

Yet darkness is

all around you

mona saudi

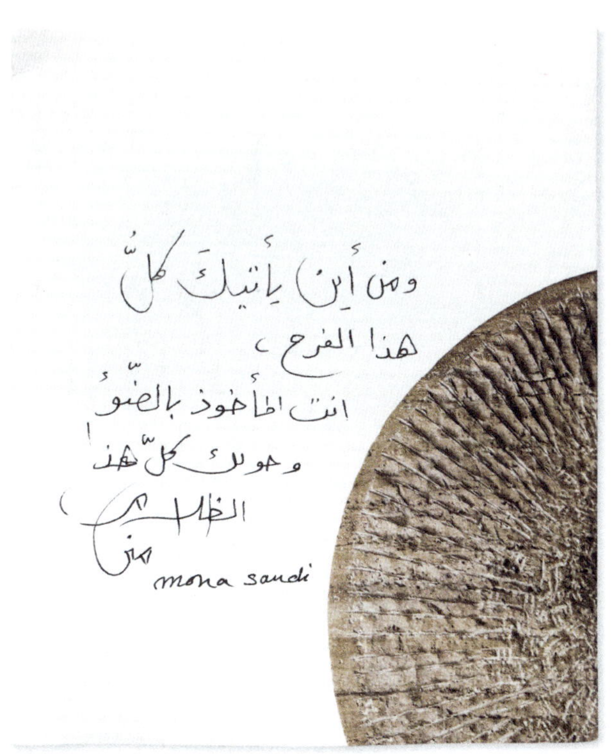
ومن أين يأتيك كل
هذا الفرح
أنت المأخوذ بالضوء
وحولك كل هذا
الظلام
منى
mona saudi

MONA SAUDI

for a better fruit, for a better life

The tree to be watered,

M.M.M. H Sebidi 2/7/2013 .

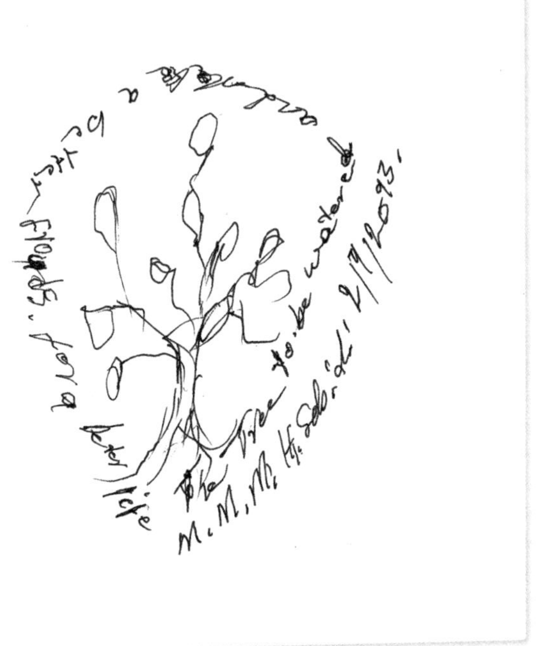

HELEN SEBIDI

I went to the

fish market, 16-3-16

afterwards I went to the

vegetable market,

then I came home without having
bought neither fish nor vegetables.

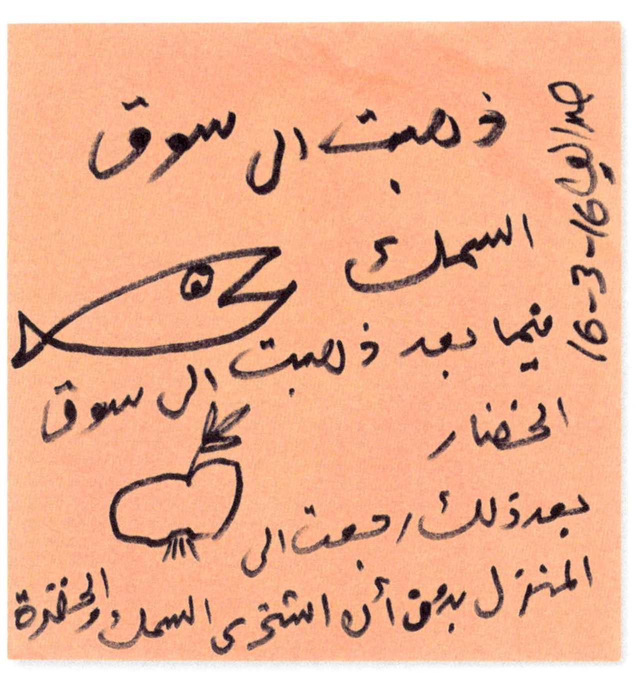

HASSAN SHARIF

Everyday
is the
best day of your

Life.

Amy Sherald

Everyday
is the
best day of your
Life.
Amy Sherald

AMY SHERALD

Not forgetting that architecture
is a service rendered to a person or to a community,
to face the need of liberation
of immediate conditioning
to conjugate service and liberty in the conquest of beauty

Álvaro Siza

Não esquecendo que a Arquitectura
é um serviço prestado a um ou a uns,
enfrentar a necessidade de libertação
dos condicionamentos imediatos
conjugar serviço e liberdade na conquista da Beleza

Álvaro Siza

ÁLVARO SIZA

ONE DAY AT A TIME

NEVER RUSH

ONE DAY AT A TIME

NEVER RUSH

SKEPTA

Mycelium is the Neural Internet of Earth

Paul Stamets

Mycelium is the
Neural Internet of Earth

Paul Stamets

PAUL STAMETS

Dull Not To

Tilda Swinton

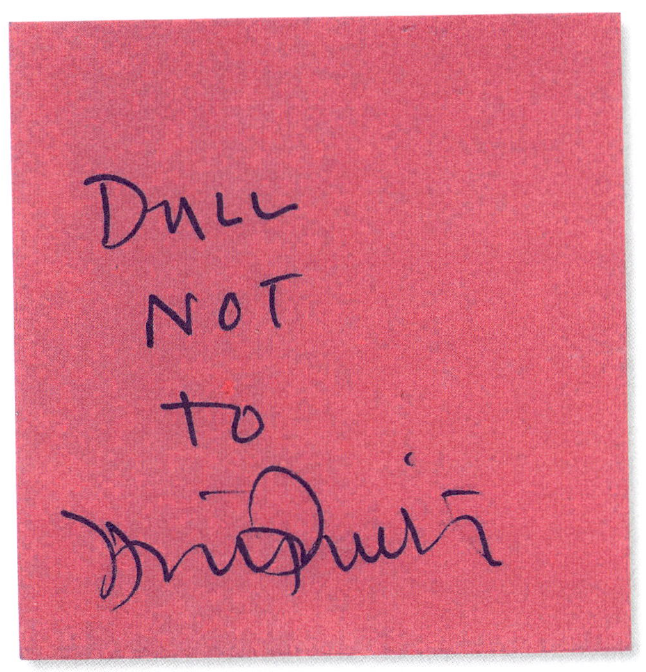

TILDA SWINTON

OH,   iF ONLy
I   COULD
LiSTEN

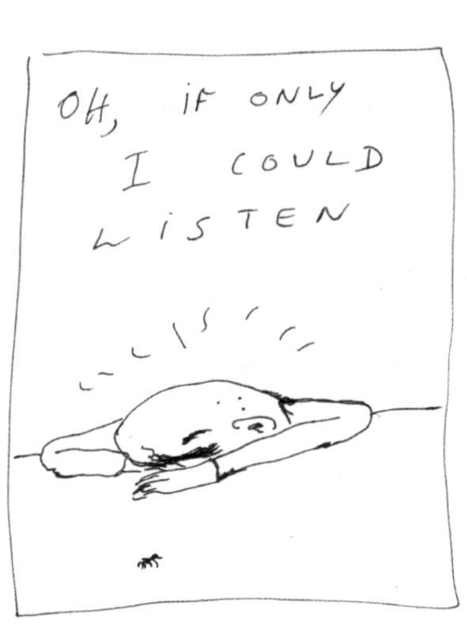

POL TABURET

love can't be

controlled

Tadáskía

O amor não
se pode
controlar

love can't be
controlled

Tadáskía

TADÁSKÍA

be enthusiastic

9. 03. 14

juergen teller

be enthusiastic

9.03.14

juergen teller

JUERGEN TELLER

Possibilities of a Structure

E TERRAZAS

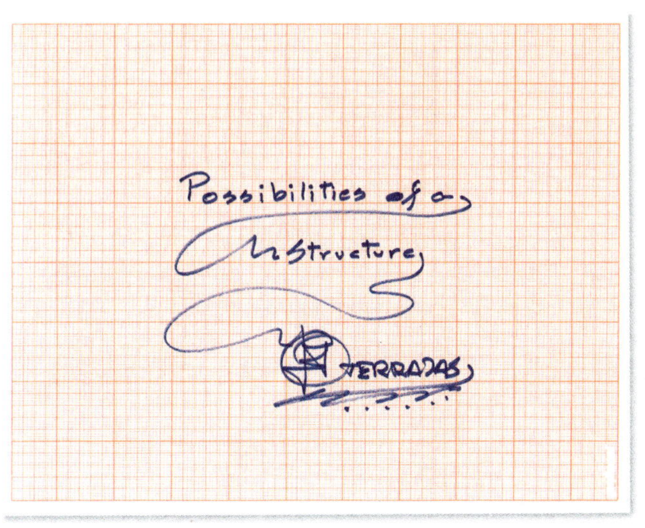

EDUARDO TERRAZAS

anthro'apology Tours

we buy and sell
origin stories

~ any condition

~ any situation

fast and easy
we have cache

for$_e$closure

anthro'apology Tours

we buy and sell
origin stories

~any condition
~any situation

fast and easy
We have cache

for$eclosure

RYAN TRECARTIN

I

die

later

Rosemarie Trockel

I

die

Luter

Rom Inucht

ROSEMARIE TROCKEL

" "Men should observe only reality, which is far more fabulous than the illusions they think are truth. "

Henry David Thoreau

via
Frederic Tuten

"Men should observe only reality, which is far more fabulous than the illusions they think are truth."

Henry David Thoreau

via

Frederic Tuten

FREDERIC TUTEN

Language is
the destruction of artists

Sprache ist
künstlervernichtung

GÜNTHER UECKER

THERE·ARE·NO·MORE·WORDS

Valcárcel Medina

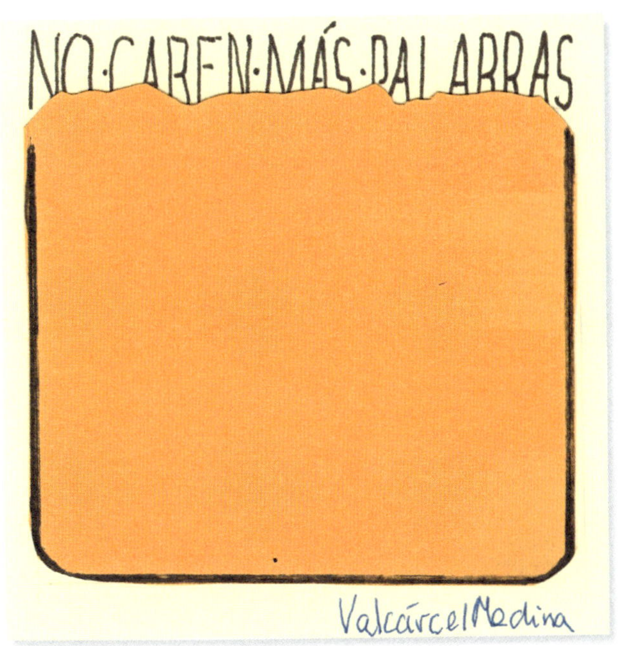

ISIDORO VALCÁRCEL MEDINA

Hopelessness is only

economical + convenient

in the short term ·

The hard work of hope

produces liberation.

Hopelessness is only economical + convenient in the short term.

The hard work of hope produces liberation.

SUMAYYA VALLY

The future

is

the past with

a

NEW DRESS.

F.V.

The future
is
the past with
a
NEW DRESS.
F.V.

FRANCESCO VEZZOLI

FACTSMATTER

wikitribune

Jimmy Wales

#FACTSMATTER

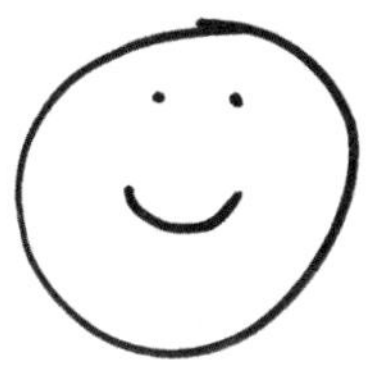

wikiTribune

Jimmy Wales

JIMMY WALES

SIX FUZZY BEAVERS

quickly jumped the narrow gap.

John Waters

Six Fuzzy Beavers
Quickly jumped the narrow gap.
John Waters

JOHN WATERS

Ich schreibe ..

I write ..

J ' écris ...

Deshalb

Therefore

alors ....

You read !

Wim Wenders

11.7.2017

Ich schreibe..
I write..
J'écris...
Das heißt
therefore
aber...
You read!

11.7.2017

WIM WENDERS

YOUTH → NEVER LOOK BACK ☆

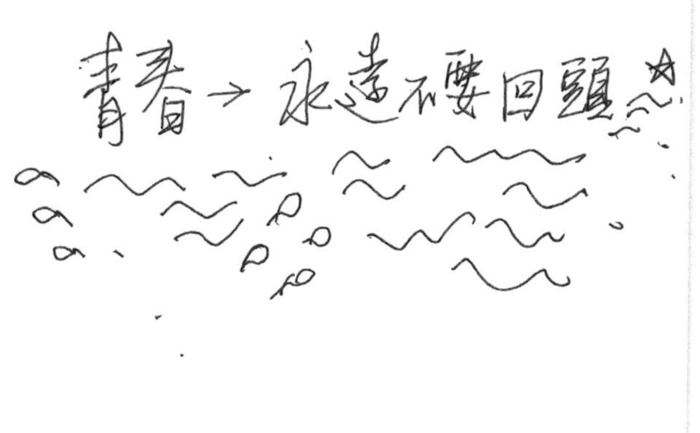

YANG FUDONG

This publication is thanks to HENI Publishing and my friend Joe Hage, who first had the idea to realise this book, and to its designer Irma Boom, who designed our book *Project Japan: Metabolism Talks* with Rem Koolhaas. I am delighted that this new project has come to fruition. Thank you to all the artists who participated in the handwriting project.

ISBN 978-1-912122-97-4

 A catalogue record for this book is available from the British Library.

Designed by Irma Boom

Printed in Italy by Graphicom

Publisher: HENI Publishing, London, United Kingdom

EU Authorised Representative: Easy Access System Europe – Mustamäe tee 50
10621 Tallinn, Estonia
gpsr.requests@easproject.com

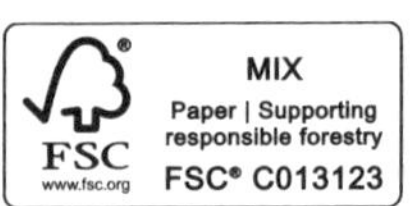